Little People, **BIG DREAMS**™

LOUISE BOURGEOIS

Written by
Maria Isabel Sánchez Vegara

Illustrated by
Helena Pérez García

Frances Lincoln
Children's Books

One Christmas day in Paris, a little girl was born.
Her name was Louise. She was not the gift-
wrapped boy her father had wanted her to be,
but her mother loved her very much.

Every day after school, Louise helped at the family tapestry studio, where huge pieces of fabric were dyed and sewn. Her mother asked her to help by filling in a missing section of tapestry. Here, Louise learned to draw legs and feet.

One day, her mother became ill. Louise
was terribly upset. She realized that painting was
the only way to let go of her fear and anger.

After her mother died, Louise decided to study art. Her father refused to support her, so Louise found a way to pay for her studies, translating art classes into English for American students.

The famous painter Fernand Léger visited her school, and Louise took the chance to show him her work. He was impressed by her eye for shapes and gave her some great advice: Louise should become a sculptor.

Louise opened a small gallery, which was always full of art lovers. One of them was Robert, an art history professor at New York University. Talking about the latest trends, they fell in love.

Louise and Robert moved to New York. From the roof of her home, she saw huge skyscrapers that inspired her to create her first sculptures: lonely people made of wood.

Every night when her children went to bed, Louise kept working on sculptures inspired by her childhood memories. They were quite strange and looked more like a nightmare than a happy dream.

Some of them were even scary! But for those who
didn't know her, Louise looked just like a charming lady
who loved to visit art exhibitions on the arm of her husband.

Louise was 70 when the Museum of Modern Art in New York finally honored her work. People found the show shocking and disturbing, but couldn't take their eyes off her sculptures.

She went on to create huge cages, filled with strange objects she had collected throughout her life. They were dark and creepy, and it took courage for someone to dare to look inside.

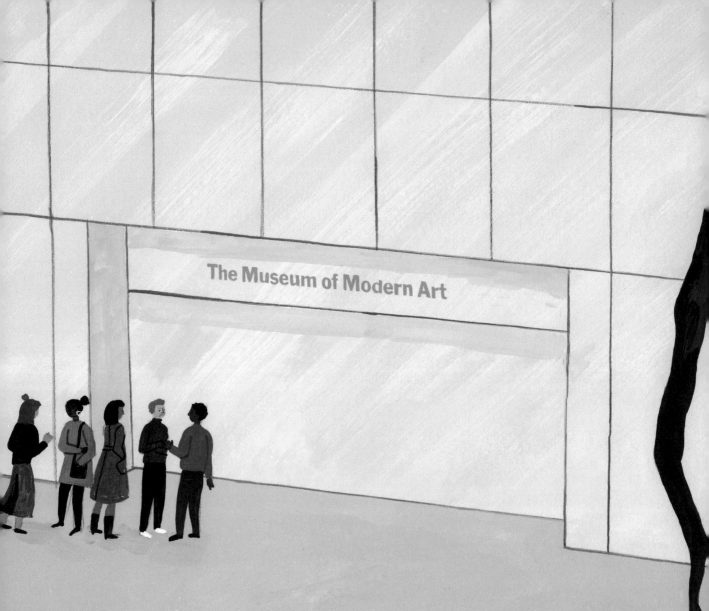

The Museum of Modern Art

To celebrate her 80th birthday, Louise brought giant spiders to museums around the world. People felt like tiny ants next to them...but not her. They reminded her of her loving mother, mending clothes at her tapestry studio.

By using art to confront her fears, little Louise became one of the most important artists of the twentieth century, and the grandmother of modern art.

LOUISE BOURGEOIS

(Born 1911 • Died 2010)

1963

1978

Born on a snowy Christmas day in 1911, Louise arrived to parents
Louis and Josephine in their house on Boulevard Saint Germain,
Paris. Louise's little brother, Pierre, was born two years later, and
before long, the family moved to a suburb just outside of Paris,
where her mother ran a tapestry-restoration workshop. Around
this time, Louise's mother became sick with the Spanish flu. Louise
spent a lot of her childhood caring for her mother, who was also
her best friend and biggest supporter. Louise's feelings of loss
in these years would become the foundation for her work as an
artist. When she went to college in Paris, she quickly became a
talented painter and printmaker. A teacher there, Fernand Léger,

1993

2017

saw something special in her work. He encouraged her to explore her work as three-dimensional objects, in sculptures. Moving to New York in 1945 with her husband, Robert, Louise began to create sculptures using old wood found on the roof of her apartment. This was just the beginning of her 60-year career, and the start of her story as the world's leading sculptor. Her retrospective at the Metropolitan Museum of Art in New York in 1982 was the first one devoted to a female artist. It was also the moment when the world sat up and watched Louise explore what it meant for women to be subjects—rather than objects—of art. Her bravery and passion for self-expression paved the way for modern artists and art lovers alike.

Want to find out more about **Louise Bourgeois?**
Read this great book:

Cloth Lullaby: The Woven Life of Louise Bourgeois
by Isabelle Arsenault

Brimming with creative inspiration, how-to
projects, and useful information to enrich your
everyday life, quarto.com is a favorite destination
for those pursuing their interests and passions.

Text copyright © 2020 Maria Isabel Sánchez Vegara. Illustrations copyright © 2020 Helena Pérez García.
Original concept of the series by Maria Isabel Sánchez Vegara, published by Alba Editorial, S.L.U.
Little People Big Dreams and Pequeña & Grande are registered trademarks of Alba Editorial, S.L.U. for books,
publications, and e-books. Produced under license from Alba Editorial, S.L.U.

First published in the US in 2020 by Frances Lincoln Children's Books, an imprint of The Quarto Group.
100 Cummings Center, Suite 265D, Beverly, MA 01915, USA.
T +1 978-282-9590 **www.quarto.com**
First Published in Spain in 2020 under the title Pequeña & Grande Louise Bourgeois
by Alba Editorial, S.L.U., Baixada de Sant Miquel, 1, 08002 Barcelona, Spain. www.albaeditorial.es
All rights reserved.

A CIP record for this book is available from the Library of Congress.
ISBN 978-0-7112-4690-4
eISBN 978-0-7112-5496-1
Set in Futura BT.

Published by Katie Cotton • Designed by Karissa Santos
Edited by Rachel Williams and Katy Flint • Production by Caragh McAleenan

Manufactured in Guangdong, China CC052022
9 7 5 4 6 8

Photographic acknowledgments (pages 28–29, from left to right) 1. 1963 - Bourgeois & Goldwater At MoMA. Photo by Fred W.
McDarrah/Getty Images 2. 1978 - Louise Bourgeois & 'Confrontation'. Photo by Fred W. McDarrah/Getty Images 3. 1993 - French
Sculptor Louise Bourgeois. Photo by Catherine Cabrol/Kipa/Sygma via Getty Images 4. 2017 - Spider sculpture outside Canadian
National Art Gallery in Ottawa. UlyssePixel / Alamy Stock Photo

Collect the *Little People*, **BIG DREAMS**™ series:

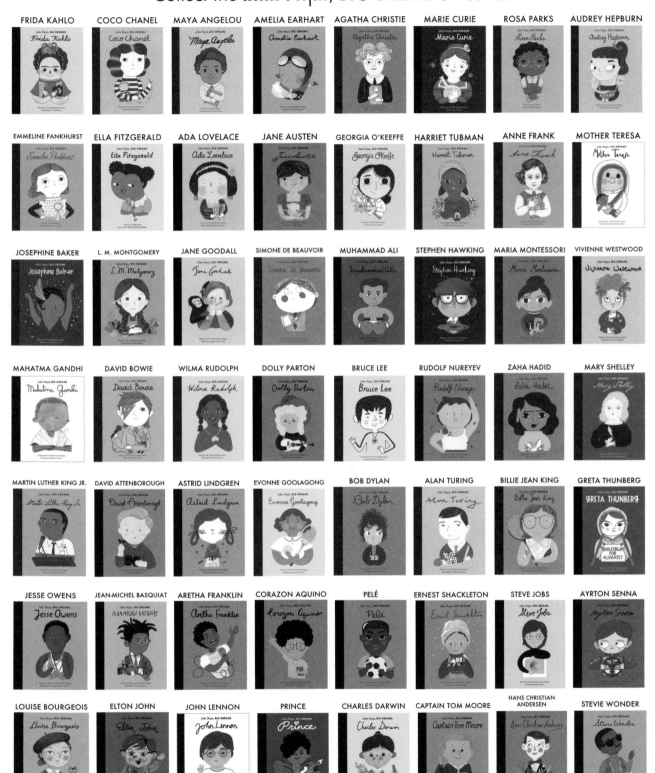

FRIDA KAHLO — COCO CHANEL — MAYA ANGELOU — AMELIA EARHART — AGATHA CHRISTIE — MARIE CURIE — ROSA PARKS — AUDREY HEPBURN

EMMELINE PANKHURST — ELLA FITZGERALD — ADA LOVELACE — JANE AUSTEN — GEORGIA O'KEEFFE — HARRIET TUBMAN — ANNE FRANK — MOTHER TERESA

JOSEPHINE BAKER — L. M. MONTGOMERY — JANE GOODALL — SIMONE DE BEAUVOIR — MUHAMMAD ALI — STEPHEN HAWKING — MARIA MONTESSORI — VIVIENNE WESTWOOD

MAHATMA GANDHI — DAVID BOWIE — WILMA RUDOLPH — DOLLY PARTON — BRUCE LEE — RUDOLF NUREYEV — ZAHA HADID — MARY SHELLEY

MARTIN LUTHER KING JR. — DAVID ATTENBOROUGH — ASTRID LINDGREN — EVONNE GOOLAGONG — BOB DYLAN — ALAN TURING — BILLIE JEAN KING — GRETA THUNBERG

JESSE OWENS — JEAN-MICHEL BASQUIAT — ARETHA FRANKLIN — CORAZON AQUINO — PELÉ — ERNEST SHACKLETON — STEVE JOBS — AYRTON SENNA

LOUISE BOURGEOIS — ELTON JOHN — JOHN LENNON — PRINCE — CHARLES DARWIN — CAPTAIN TOM MOORE — HANS CHRISTIAN ANDERSEN — STEVIE WONDER

MEGAN RAPINOE

MARY ANNING

MALALA YOUSAFZAI

ANDY WARHOL

RUPAUL

MICHELLE OBAMA

MINDY KALING

IRIS APFEL

ROSALIND FRANKLIN

RUTH BADER GINSBURG

MARILYN MONROE

KAMALA HARRIS

ALBERT EINSTEIN

CHARLES DICKENS

YOKO ONO

MICHAEL JORDAN

NELSON MANDELA

PABLO PICASSO

AMANDA GORMAN

GLORIA STEINEM

FLORENCE NIGHTINGALE

HARRY HOUDINI

J.R.R. TOLKIEN

ELVIS PRESLEY

NEIL ARMSTRONG

ALEXANDER VON HUMBOLDT

NIKOLA TESLA

WILMA MANKILLER

MARCUS RASHFORD

ACTIVITY BOOKS

STICKER ACTIVITY BOOK

COLORING BOOK

LITTLE ME, BIG DREAMS JOURNAL

Discover more about the series at www.littlepeoplebigdreams.com